CONQUERING MOUNT EVEREST

BY JACKIE GLASSMAN

Table of Contents

On Top of the World

"**W**e look up. For weeks, for months, that is all we have done. Look up. And there it is–the top of Everest. Only it is different now: so near, so close, only a little more than a thousand feet above us. It is no longer just a dream, a high dream in the sky, but a real and solid thing, a thing of rock and snow that men can climb."

> – *Tenzing Norgay,*
> *Tiger of the Snows*

←
Tenzing Norgay plants an ice ax covered with flags into Everest's icy summit.

↑
Edmund Hillary (left) and Tenzing Norgay (right) take a break during their expedition.

On May 29, 1953, after months of trekking through ice and snow, Tenzing Norgay saw his dream come true. He and Edmund Hillary became the first people ever to reach the top of Mount Everest.

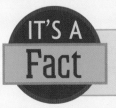
IT'S A
Fact

In 1958, Edmund Hillary went to the South Pole.

Standing at 29,028 feet, or five and a half miles above sea level, Mount Everest is the highest mountain in the world. It is part of the **Himalayan mountain range**. The mountain straddles the border between Nepal and Tibet. Tibet is a region of China.

Long ago, there were no Himalayan mountains. Instead, there was an ocean between India and Asia. Then, 40 million years ago, India crashed into the Asian continent, pushing up the Himalayas as it moved. Believe it or not, India is still moving two inches a year, making the mountains even taller!

HOW DID MOUNT EVEREST GET ITS NAME?

In the 1820s, an Englishman named Sir George Everest was the first to record the location and height of the mountain, then known as Peak 15. It was renamed in Everest's honor.

35,000 feet

29,028 feet
Top of Mount Everest

IT'S A
Fact

**How tall is
29,028 feet?**

Mount Everest is
the same height as
almost 24 Empire
State Buildings!

That's almost as
high as a jet flies.

1,250 feet
Top of
Empire State
Building

Climbing Everest

Reaching Everest's peak is not easy. Climbers face bitter cold winds while trekking through heavy snow. Deep **crevasses** in the ice open and close all the time, making the climb very dangerous.

Then there is the blowing snow, which makes it difficult to see, even just a few feet ahead. Powerful winds have actually blown climbers right off the mountainside! **Avalanches**, moving at speeds of 200 miles per hour, are the biggest killers of all.

The higher up climbers go, the less air there is to breathe. Climbers must make several trips from base **camp** to higher and higher camps on the mountain until their bodies get used to the lack of oxygen.

At the top of Everest, there is only one-third as much oxygen as at sea level. Most (but not all) climbers need extra oxygen.

Upon reaching the summit, climbers can stay for only a few moments. If they stay any longer, the lack of oxygen can weaken them, making the trek down difficult.

↑ An avalanche sends snow down the side of a mountain in the Himalayas.

→ This climber is wearing an oxygen mask and has a lamp on his head to help him climb in the dark.

IT'S A Fact

An avalanche is snowfall that builds up on a mountainside and then breaks off, sliding down the mountain at high speeds.

GET IN GEAR

Oxygen is just one item climbers need to make the trek. Here are more. Can you match each picture with its description? (See page 32 for answers.)

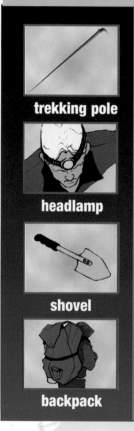

trekking pole

headlamp

shovel

backpack

1. Sharp metal spikes to walk on ice

2. Use this for balance

3. Cuts footholds in the ice

4. Carries food, equipment, and clothes

5. Climbers attach themselves to these for safety

6. Digs out climbers buried by avalanches

7. This outermost layer keeps climbers warm at temperatures near -100° Fahrenheit

8. Climbers wear this for trekking at night

climbing suit

ropes

crampon

ice ax

Don't like the cold? Then mountain climbing is not for you. On Mount Everest, nighttime temperatures can drop to as low as –100° Fahrenheit!

Climbers risk getting **frostbite**—that's when a body gets so cold that it freezes. In extreme cases, frostbite can result in the loss of a finger or toe.

This Mount Everest climber displays his frostbitten fingers.

Between avalanches, frostbite, lack of oxygen, and other dangers, why would anyone want to climb Mount Everest? In the words of British climber George Mallory, "Because it's there."

CHAPTER 3

The Sherpas

For many people, Mount Everest is more than rocks, snow, and ice. The **Sherpas**, natives to the Himalayan region, have always thought that the mountain is holy. They call it "Chomolungma," which means "Mother Goddess of the Earth," because they believe it is the home of the gods. Before the early 1900s, no Sherpas climbed the mountain because of this belief.

Born and raised on the mountains, Sherpas are skilled climbers. Famous for their physical strength at high **altitudes**, they have guided other climbers since the earliest Everest **expeditions**.

Sherpas are Buddhists who moved from Tibet to Nepal several hundred years ago. Stones with Buddhist prayers written on them line Everest's trails. These prayers remind climbers that the mountain should be treated like a holy place.

↑ This is a modern-day Sherpa on Mount Everest.

The Tengboche (teng-BOTCH) Monastery is one of the most important religious centers in Sherpa culture. Here monks perform Mani Rimdu, a masked dance ceremony in which they ask the gods for protection during the climb.

IT'S A
Fact

Sherpas make up one-quarter of the total number of people climbing Everest. They also account for one-third of the lives lost on the mountain.

Tengboche Monastery

The Early Everest Explorers

Sherpas are not the only ones to admire Mount Everest. For years, people all over the world wanted to be the first to plant their country's flag on its peak. Many died trying.

George Mallory from Britain led the earliest organized attempt to climb Everest in 1921. Overcome by illness, exhaustion, and bad weather, the explorers never made it to the top, but they did find a route to the summit.

Determined to conquer Everest, Mallory returned to the mountain in 1922. He still could not make it to the top. In addition, his team, walking slowly through heavy snow, set off an avalanche, killing seven Sherpas.

During his third and final attempt in 1924, something went wrong again. High on Everest's slopes, Mallory and a team member vanished only 800 feet from the summit! Their disappearance remains one of mountain climbing's greatest mysteries to this day.

→

Here is a photo of the 1921 expedition team. Mallory is in the front row on the far left.

The first explorers approached Mount Everest from the Tibet side on the north. Today, most expeditions climb from the Nepal side on the south.

In 1996, Mallory's body was discovered on Everest, seventy-five years after disappearing. The clues left behind, however, don't reveal what happened. No one even knows whether he reached the summit before he died.

↑
Mallory and a companion climb Mount Everest in 1922.

"We make ready. We will climb it. This time, with God's help, we will climb on to the end." — *Tenzing Norgay*

For many years after Mallory's death, climbers tried to reach the top of Everest, but it wasn't until 1953 that anybody would stand on the "roof of the world."

In that year, another British team arrived in the Himalayas. Sixteen days after leaving Katmandu on foot, Edmund Hillary of New Zealand, Tenzing Norgay of Nepal, and the rest of the British team reached the base of the mountain. After trekking 170 miles, they were still only at the bottom!

Pushing on, Hillary led some of the team up one of the steepest and most dangerous parts of the climb, the Khumbu (KOOM-boo) Icefall.

Roped together, Hillary and Norgay cut through deep ice, making their way around hidden crevasses. After establishing a camp at 27,900 feet, the rest of the team went back down the mountain, leaving the two men to make the final **ascent** on their own.

Faced with a forty-foot vertical snow cliff, they used every ounce of energy to work their way up. Hour after hour, the men cut steps into the ice, pulling themselves over ridge after ridge, until finally there was no more mountain to climb. They had done it! Hillary and Norgay were on top of the world.

→ **Hillary (left) and Norgay (right) prepare to leave a camp.**

14

The Khumbu Icefall is a glacier that flows over a very steep part of the mountain. The glacier moves a couple of feet every day, making the climb up it very scary.

Disaster Strikes!

ay 10, 1996, marks the date of one of the most tragic events in mountain climbing history. On that day, snow, bitter cold, and hurricane-force winds swept through Everest's highest peaks as thirty-three climbers tried to get down the mountain.

American team ↓

There were at least three teams planning to go to the summit that day. Two of the teams, one from New Zealand and one from the United States, were the largest on the mountain. This meant that a lot of people would be climbing up Everest's icy, narrow trails at the same time.

↑ New Zealand team

The climbers from these teams began their trek to the top of the mountain around midnight. The weather was mild.

Trekking through the dark by the light of headlamps, the climbers hoped to reach the summit by noon. That way, they would have plenty of time to get down the mountain before nightfall.

**This map shows the route →
taken by the American and
New Zealand teams.**

Summit 29,923 feet

Camp IV
26,000 feet

Camp III
24,500 feet

Camp II
21,300 feet

Camp I
19,900 feet

Base Camp
17,700 feet

Just after 1 p.m., John Krakauer, a member of the New Zealand team, reached a lifelong goal as he took his final steps up to the highest point on Earth.

But instead of excitement, he felt cold, tired, and very nervous about the long and dangerous trek back down the mountain.

Mount Everest ↓

THINK IT OVER!

A mere 200 feet below the peak, the Hillary Step is one of the most difficult parts of the climb. Imagine you are one of the climbers waiting on line. It's getting cloudy, your oxygen is running low, and it's brutally cold. How would you feel? Write about it.

Spending less than five minutes on the summit, Krakauer began his climb down. Reaching the top of the Hillary Step, forty vertical feet of ice and rock leading down from the summit, he was surprised to see over a dozen climbers from all three teams, standing at the base of the Hillary Step. They were waiting to climb up the fixed rope.

By this late hour, climbers usually turn around if they haven't reached the top. For many, however, this was a dream of a lifetime, and they were not willing to give up.

Since so many climbers were still scaling the step, Krakauer would have to wait to go down.

The American team ascends the Hillary Step. ➔

Climbers make their way up
Mount Everest on May 10, 1996.

They'd be fatigued, out of oxygen and descending in he dark. Things did not look good." —*David Breashears*

Krakauer wasn't the only one who was concerned. From a lower camp, David Breashears, he leader of a team that was ilming an Everest trek, peered hrough his telescope. Watching he climbers inching up the mountain, he worried whether or not their bottled oxygen vould get them to the summit and back to camp safely.

An hour later, with growing concern, Breashears checked again only to discover that the climbers had hardly moved.

The climbers Krakauer had seen at the Hillary Step earlier finally reached the summit. Though it was late afternoon, they celebrated their success, planting flags, snapping photos, and not worrying about the climb down.

The sun was still shining and the sky was clear. They did not realize that far below a brutal blizzard was brewing. In just a few hours, it would hit the mountain full force, attacking each camp on its way up the mountain until it reached the climbers at the top.

These climbers reached the summit of Mount Everest before the blizzard struck.

Scott Fischer, the leader of the American team took this photo as climbers descended Mount Everest.

As late as 4:00 p.m., Rob Hall, the leader of the New Zealand team, was helping Doug Hansen up the final forty feet to the summit. The rest of the New Zealand team went down the mountain without their leader. As the clouds grew darker and the wind picked up, it became harder to see and the team quickly became separated.

On his way back down the mountain, Hansen collapsed. Hall got on the radio to say that they were in trouble and that they needed oxygen.

As the evening wore on, the blizzard grew stronger. Seventy-mile-per-hour bitter cold winds worked against the climbers as they made their way down. The falling snow made it impossible to see more than just a few feet ahead.

Of the thirty-three people who had set out for Everest's peak that day, nineteen were stranded on the mountain, struggling for their lives.

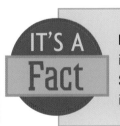

IT'S A Fact

Hypoxia, or shortage of oxygen at high altitude, is one of the biggest dangers the climbers faced. Some doctors believe extreme hypoxia may result in brain damage.

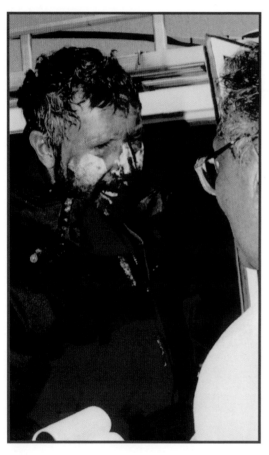

↑
Seaborn Beck Weathers, a survivor of the 1996 Mount Everest expedition, talks to journalists after being rescued.

Throughout the evening, a handful of climbers made it back to camp, including Krakauer. Severely frostbitten and needing oxygen, some were in danger of losing their lives.

Finally, in the early hours of the morning, as the storm was dying down, Rob Hall's voice came over the base-camp radio. Doug Hansen had died, and Hall, still high up on the mountain, was in bad shape.

As the hours wore on, there were reports of more dead and injured climbers. Though Hall survived overnight and into the next day, he was simply too high up to be rescued. He, too, died in the snow and ice.

In the end, the blizzard claimed the lives of eight brave adventurers, including two of the world's top climbing-team leaders. It was a very sad day in mountain-climbing history.

The leaders of both the New Zealand and American teams died on the mountain. Rob Hall (left) was the New Zealand team leader. Scott Fischer (inset) was the American team leader.

Everybody's Everest

Mount Everest is more accessible today than ever before. More than fifty years since the first climb to the top, climbers can now call home from the summit. They can send e-mail. They can choose from among many different trained guides to lead them to the top.

But don't be mistaken. Everest is still a challenge. Climbers must be physically and mentally prepared. Reaching the highest point in the world is the reward for years of hard work and planning.

What makes Everest so magical? Why are mountaineers so eager to climb it even though one in every thirty people dies on the mountain? For one determined climber, Jamling Tenzing Norgay, son of Tenzing Norgay, reaching the top was the fulfillment of a childhood dream.

"I've always had this urge to climb Everest. Since I was 18 years old I wanted to climb but my father said no. He said 'Why do you want to climb? I already climbed it for you.'"

In 1996, Jamling's dream came true. It was every bit as wonderful as he'd hoped.

"The moment I reached the summit I felt a rush of excitement. This was where my father had stood 43 years ago.... I cried a bit out of joy, and as I looked around, I put my hands together and said 'thu chi-chay'—thank you—to Chomolungma."

Climbers celebrate after reaching the peak of Everest.

THINK IT OVER!

Considering all of the dangers involved, would you ever want to try to conquer Everest? Why or why not?

MOUNT EVEREST RECORDS

First climb:
Edmund Hillary (New Zealand)
& Tenzing Norgay (Nepal) in 1953

Oldest climber:
Toshio Yamamoto (Japan),
63 years old, in 2000

First climb by a woman:
Junko Tabei (Japan)
in 1975

Youngest climber:
Shambu Tamang (Nepal),
6 years old, in 1973

First oxygenless climb:
Reinhold Messner (Austria) &
Peter Habeler (Austria) in 1978

Fastest climb:
Hans Kammerlander (Italy),
6 hours and 45 minutes, in 1996

First solo climb:
Reinhold Messner (Austria)
in 1980

Most climbs:
Appa Sherpa (Nepal), 11 times

Glossary

altitude   (AL-tih-tood) the height of an object above sea level

ascent   (uh-SENT) the act of rising or climbing up

avalanche   (A-vuh-lanch) the sudden movement of a large mass of snow, ice, or rock down a mountainside

camp   (KAMP) a central setup of tents where food, equipment, and medical supplies are stored; a relay site for climbers

crampon   (KRAM-pahn) metal frame with spikes worn on hiking boots for climbing on ice

crevasses   (krih-VAS-ez) deep, open cracks in a glacier

expedition   (ek-speh-DIH-shun) a journey or trip undertaken for a specific purpose

frostbite   (FRAUST-bite) the freezing or partial freezing of some part of the body

Himalayan mountain range   (hih-muh-LAY-un MOWN-tun RANJE) the highest mountain range in the world, rising between India and China

hypoxia   (hy-PAHK-see-uh) a deficiency of oxygen in the tissues of the body that causes lightheadedness and other symptoms

Sherpas   (SHER-puz) people who moved from Tibet to the Everest area of Nepal hundreds of years ago

summit   (SUH-mit) the highest point, as on a mountain

Index

Answers for page 8:
1. crampon
2. trekking pole
3. ice ax
4. backpack
5. ropes
6. shovel
7. climbing suit
8. headlamp